Lost & Found

By Nancy I. Sanders
and Susan Titus Osborn

Illustrated by Julie Durrell

With love for my granddaughter Taylor.
May you learn more about Jesus
through reading this book. — S.T.O.

With love for Janice and Bob Shaner.
Thanks for your example of living
and knowing Jesus. — N.I.S.

Parables in Action Series

Lost and Found
Hidden Treasure
Comet Campout
Moon Rocks and Dinosaur Bones

Text copyright © 1999 Nancy I. Sanders and Susan Titus Osborn
Illustrations copyright © 1999 Concordia Publishing House
3558 S. Jefferson Avenue, St. Louis, MO 63118-3968
Manufactured in the United States of America

1 2 3 4 5 6 7 8 9 10   08 07 06 05 04 03 02 01 00 99

Hi! My name is Suzie. Our
class is going on a field trip today.
We are going to a sea animal park.
Sharks, sea lions, whales, and
penguins live there. Most of all,
I want to see the octopus.

"Everyone find a buddy," said Mr. Zinger, our teacher. "I don't want anyone to get lost."

My friend, Mario, chose The Spy for his buddy. I chose Bubbles. Her real name is Nan. She is on TV and does ads for juice and toys. One time I saw her picture on a jar of bubbles at the store. We all called her Bubbles after that.

"Why are you dressed like a clown?" I asked.

"It's for my next TV ad, Suzie," said Bubbles. "I'm practicing to be a circus clown on TV."

Bubbles stood on her head. She fell over and giggled. All the kids laughed.

Our bus drove up. Bubbles and I hopped up the stairs. We sat down on the hard seats. Ouch! Bubbles jumped up again. Everyone laughed.

Mr. Zinger climbed on the bus. He counted everyone. "… 58, 59, 60. We're all here—all 60 kids. Let's go!"

The bus bumped up and down on the road. We bumped up and down on the seats.

Mr. Zinger played his guitar. Mr. Zinger's the best! First we sang "If You're Happy and You Know It, Clap Your Hands." Then we made up new verses like "If you love Jesus and you know it, shout hooray." Or "If you're a friend and you know it, snap your fingers."

While we sang, Bubbles practiced. She made funny clown faces. She pulled her red nose. SNAP! It snapped on her face. Bubbles pretended to cry. Everyone laughed.

Mario and The Spy sat in front of us. The Spy didn't watch Mario. He didn't watch Bubbles. The Spy didn't laugh. He wrote in a little book.

I stopped singing. I peeked in his book. The Spy closed his book. SLAM!

"Writing spy notes?" I asked.

The Spy whispered in my ear. "Iggle, iggle, snoogle, snoogle."

I knew what he said. I'd been around The Spy a long time. "Iggle, iggle, snoogle, snoogle" was his secret code for "yes." The Spy always wrote spy notes. He liked to talk in secret code.

The bus stopped in front of the sea animal park. "Hip, hip, hooray!" we all cheered.

Everyone marched off the bus. We stood in a lo-o-ong line. Mr. Zinger counted us. "... 58, 59, 60," he said. "We're all here—all 60 kids. Let's go!"

We hiked up the sidewalk. We passed a toy store and a snack shop. A zoo guide met us at the park gate.

"Come look at the sea animals," he said. "Our first stop is the octopus tank."

"The octopus is my favorite!"
I said.

We walked into the building
and up to the octopus tank.

"Oh, no!" the guide cried.
"Where is the octopus?"

The tank looked empty. "The
octopus pulled the stopper!"
said the guide. "He reached out
one of his arms and opened the
tank. He escaped!"

Suddenly bells rang.
CLANG! CLANG! CLANG!

Workers ran everywhere.
Water dripped on the floor.

The Spy wrote lots of spy notes.

Bubbles slipped on the wet floor. SPLASH!

Mr. Zinger tripped over her big clown shoes. CRASH!

The zoo guide yelled, "Help! Help! Help find the octopus!"

I said a quick prayer. I asked Jesus to help us.

One of the workers ran past me.

"Can I help clean up?" I shouted.

"There isn't time to clean up now!" he cried.

The zoo worker slipped and fell.

Shouts were heard everywhere. "We must find the octopus!"

"Boys! Girls!" Mr. Zinger shouted. "Class! Stop!"

Nobody listened to him. Everyone ran everywhere! Mr. Zinger blew his whistle.

T-W-E-E-E-T!

Suddenly we all stopped. We HAD to stop when we heard that whistle.

"Let's stay out of the workers' way," Mr. Zinger said. "Let's go look at the tide pool."

Everyone walked over to the tide pool.

Suddenly I screamed. "Snakes! Snakes! Look at all the snakes in the tide pool!"

The snakes moved. The snakes climbed out of the pool. The snakes ran across the floor. Now EVERYONE screamed!

"That's not a snake," the guide shouted. "That's the octopus. Catch him!"

The chase was on! All the kids tried to catch him. No one ran fast enough. The kids bumped into the workers. THUMP! The workers crashed into the kids. SMASH! Everyone fell down.

"Girls! Boys!" Mr. Zinger shouted. "Class! Stop!" He blew his whistle. T-W-E-E-E-T! We all stopped.

"Let's go outside," Mr. Zinger said. "The workers will catch the octopus."

Mr. Zinger counted us. "... 57, 58, 59," he said.

He counted us again. "... 57, 58, 59."

"Someone is missing!" I shouted. "Who could it be?"

Mr. Zinger said, "Everyone grab your buddy's hand."

I grabbed Bubbles' white clown glove. Everyone else grabbed a buddy's hand. Everyone except The Spy. The Spy was busy writing notes.

"Larry!" Mr. Zinger cried. Larry was The Spy's real name. "Larry, where is your buddy?"

The Spy looked up. He looked down. He peeked all around. He couldn't find Mario. The Spy wrote so many notes, he didn't see that his buddy was gone. Mario was missing!

"Maybe he's chasing the octopus," I said.

Mr. Zinger looked behind him. He didn't see Mario. The workers shouted. Around and around they chased the octopus.

"Let's go over to the picnic tables," said Mr. Zinger. "You kids can eat your lunch early. I'll look for Mario."

We ate our lunch and waited.

The octopus ran out one door. Three workers raced after him. The octopus ran back in another door.

We waited and waited. Mr. Zinger didn't come back.

Bubbles stood up. She practiced a flip. "Maybe Mario went swimming with the whales," she joked. Nobody laughed.

We were worried. "Maybe Mario fell in the shark tank," I said. I prayed for Mario. I asked Jesus to help us find him.

The octopus ran out the door again. Two seals raced after him. Four penguins hopped after the seals. Six workers chased all of them. "The octopus opened all the cages!" they shouted.

All the kids jumped up. We chased all the animals back into the building.

Then we sat down at the picnic tables again. We waited for Mr. Zinger. And we waited for Mario.

We sat in the sun. It was hot. "Look," I said to Bubbles. "They sell ice cream. I want an ice-cream bar."

Suddenly we heard a big cheer.

The guide peeked out the door. She shouted, "We caught the octopus and the animals! But the best news is—we found Mario!"

Mr. Zinger and Mario walked out the door. All the kids clapped and cheered. All the workers cheered too. Bubbles flipped two flips.

I said a prayer of thanks.

Mario waved.

"Hip, hip, hooray!" we all shouted.

"We put the octopus in his tank. Then we looked for a mop to clean up the mess," Mr. Zinger said. "When we opened the closet door, we found Mario. He was locked inside!"

"What a day. We're happy you found Mario," the guide said. "We'll give everyone a free ice-cream bar to celebrate."

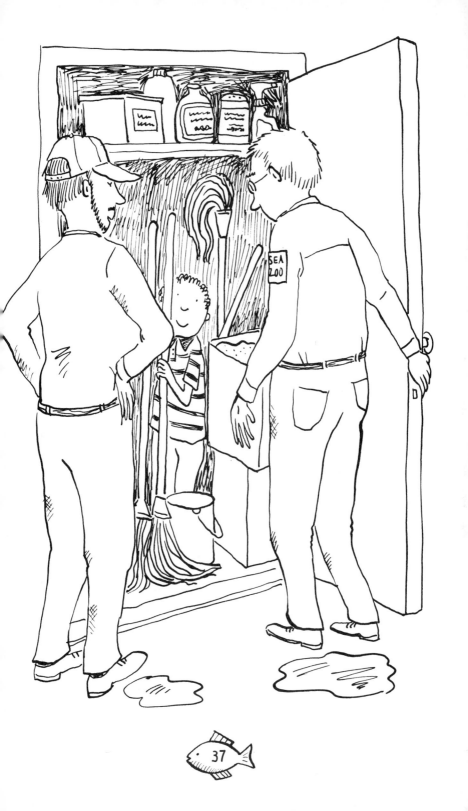

They passed out the ice-cream bars. Bubbles told jokes. "What time is it when a shark smiles at you?" she asked. "Time to jump out of the water!" We all laughed.

We finally walked through the sea animal park. We looked at the eel, the starfish, the sharks, and the octopus. The whale was super! What a dive! He splashed everyone.

"Why were you in the closet?" I asked Mario.

"I wanted to find a mop," he said. "When I looked in the closet, someone shut the door. It locked by mistake."

Mario pulled a toy shark from his pocket. "One worker gave me a gift. I'll add it to my collection." Mario likes to collect things. He has a big collection of toy fish.

Then we marched back to the bus. Mario and The Spy sat in front of us.

Mr. Zinger climbed on the bus. He counted all of us. "… 58, 59, 60. We're all here—all 60 kids. Let's go!" he said.

The bus started to move. It bumped up and down on the road.

We bumped up and down on the seats. We all turned to wave good-bye to the animals.

Everyone except The Spy. He was busy writing notes.

The park gate flew open.

Out ran the octopus. He waved.

In one arm the octopus held a sign. The sign said COME BACK SOON!

We all cheered. What a day!

Parable of the Lost Sheep

Based on Luke 15:3–7

One day, Jesus told a parable:

"What if you had one hundred sheep?" He asked. "What if one sheep got lost? What would you do?

"You would hike through the hills. When you found the lost sheep, you would put it on your shoulders. Smiling, you'd carry it home. You'd shout to your friends, 'Be happy with me! I found my lost sheep!'"

Mario was like the lost sheep. When Mr. Zinger counted the kids, "… 57, 58, 59," he knew someone was missing! When the shepherd counted his sheep, "… 97, 98, 99," he, too, knew one was missing.

46

God loves everyone so much
that He doesn't want anyone to
be lost by not knowing Jesus.
God wants everyone to be a
part of His family.

Hi, everyone! God wants all your friends to know Jesus. Here's one way you can put Jesus' Parable of the Lost Sheep into ACTION!

Parables In Action

Get Ready. Get together with other kids at church. Pray for a friend you know who doesn't go to church.

Get Set. Put things in a basket like popcorn, snacks, and a fun toy.

Go! Stop by your friend's house. Drop off the basket and invite your friend to church.